What Careers Interest You?

by Raquel Santiago

Editorial Offices: Glenview, Illinois • Parsippany, New Jersey • New York, New York
Sales Offices: Needham, Massachusetts • Duluth, Georgia • Glenview, Illinois
Coppell, Texas • Sacramento, California • Mesa, Arizona

Do you ever think about why people choose a career? Why does one person choose to be a teacher? Why does another person choose to be a doctor, or a piano player, or a car mechanic, or a gardener, or a nurse? Many people choose kinds of work they like to do.

doctor

car mechanic

---

choose: pick, select

2

teacher

Do you like to help other children with their homework? Do you like to help other students with their reading or their math? Maybe one day you will be a teacher.

People have to study to become teachers. What is the job of a teacher? Teachers help students learn math and reading. They also help students learn science, social studies, music, art, and gym. Teachers help you to get an education.

astronaut

Do you like to read books about traveling into space? Would you like to travel to the Moon? Would you like to visit other planets one day?

Maybe you can choose a career as an astronaut. Astronauts travel into space. Astronauts have to study for many years. They also have to train their bodies to be healthy and strong.

Astronauts have many chores. One chore is to fix the spacecraft when something is wrong. Another chore is to take care of the computers inside a spacecraft, or on the ground. Astronauts can work inside or outside the spacecraft.

Astronauts also carry out science experiments. For example, they can study how plants grow in space. Or they can study how animals behave in space. Astronauts help us to learn about space and planets.

---

spacecraft: vehicle that goes into space

gardener

Do you like to grow plants or flowers? Do you like to help take care of a garden? Maybe you can choose a career as a gardener.

Gardeners have to study about trees and plants. Gardeners take care of the soil. They plant flowers and trees. They know when trees are sick and how to cure them. Many gardeners also take care of lawns. Gardeners work all year around. In places where winters are cold and snowy, they do indoor work for part of the year.

---

soil: layer of the ground where plants grow

baker

Do you like to help your family make cakes and cookies? Would you like to bake bread? Maybe you can choose a career as a baker. Many bakers learn about kinds of flour for breads and cakes. They learn how to work the bakery ovens.

Bakers start work very early in the morning. They make sure bakery customers have fresh bread to eat!

Many people like the careers that they choose.

A car mechanic likes to fix cars.

An artist likes to paint.

A vet likes to take care of animals.

A bus driver likes to drive a bus.

What do you like to do?